Work Force Management

Life-changing Roles and Goals for Today's Christian Manager

By Dr. Bill McCallister

Buena Book Service

3825 Hartzdale Drive
Camp Hill, PA 17011

ISBN: 0-88965-133-7

Copyright 1996 by Bill McCallister

To Ron Ruegsegger, Ph.D.,
Academic Dean of Nyack College,
whose counsel, actions, and life choices
have convinced me that God also
builds His Kingdom through
business managers who surrender to Him.

In appreciation to Marianna Anderson
for illustrating this text with a compassionate heart for
the evangelism of fellow workers.

Contents

Foreword

By Pat Williams
General Manager of the *Orlando Magic*®

In the daily bustle of corporate life, decisions are made, employees are hired, ideas are exchanged and new enterprises begin. In completing these tasks, basic managerial principles are used. Yet, for those of us who are Christians, management goes beyond this. In the day-to-day dealings we have with people, we must be aware of how God wants us to handle every situation.

Whether it's managing a professional basketball team like the *Orlando Magic*® or managing the corner grocery store, Christian managers need to promote the Kingdom of God. This book takes management principles to a higher level, giving them the Christian perspective. Additionally, management style is as important to a work force as it is at the corporate offices of a championship basketball team. The essence of "style" is a behavioral choice that every manager, coach, or leader makes in order to direct the resources of a group of people to accomplish specific goals.

A manager who has a Christian perspective will choose the behavioral role of a peacemaker, when appropriate, and the role of a taskmaker, when assignments need to be accomplished. Knowing when to role-play one or the other is called "timing." Couple this with a compelling need to carry the gospel to the work force, and the enormous impact of any manager's chosen style becomes self-evident.

In the final analysis, what really matters is our ultimate accountability to God. When the time comes to meet our Master face-to-face He may ask us, "What have you done to lead other workers into My Kingdom?"

The time has come for all managers to "get off the bench" and score by taking the Christian perspective to the work force. If you are a Christian in a leadership role, the only way some people will ever encounter Jesus is through you—your words, your actions, your life.

This book will teach you how to role-play the activities of management, and it will help you to grasp the potential of your role as a manager. You will be challenged to make a difference for the Kingdom everyday at work. Some of the teachings in this book will sink directly in your heart! When this happens, I sincerely hope that you begin to understand and grow closer to the Redeeming Savior more and more as you journey through your management career.

There is, indeed, a Kingdom role for a peacemaker and a taskmaker with regard to work force management. Don't miss the life script that God has written especially for you.

Acknowledgments

The author is grateful for permission to use ideas, quotations and paraphrases from other sources. They are acknowledged below and further referenced as endnotes in the appropriate chapter.

Be Dynamic. Copyright © 1987. Used by permission of Victor Books, Wheaton, Ill. 60187.

Christ and the Critics. Copyright © unknown. Used by permission of Burns & Oates, LTD., Tunbridge Wells, Kent, TN2 3DR, UK.

God Owns My Business. Copyright © 1969. Used by permission of Stanley Tam, Lima, Ohio 45801.

Human Relations Concepts and Skills. Copyright © 1982. Used by permission of James M. Higgins, Winter Park, Fla. 32792.

Modern Management: Quality, Ethics, and the Global Environment, 6th edition. Copyright © 1994. Used by permission of Prentice Hall Publishers, Englewood Cliffs, NJ 07632.

The New Bible Commentary, 3rd edition. Copyright © 1970. Used by permission of Inter-Varsity Press, Leicester, LEI 7GP, UK.

The author is grateful for permission to use the substance of the following article: "Managing Attorneys' Performances by Objectives," by William McCallister, in *Law Office Economics and Management*, vol. 34, no. 1 (1993). Reprinted with permission from *Law Office Economics and Management*, Volume 34, No. 1, published by Clark Boardman Callahagan, 155 Pfingsten Road, Deerfield, Ill. 60015. Toll-free 1-800/221-9428.

Additionally, the author acknowledges gratitude for quotations and paraphrases taken from *The Ethic of Jesus*, by James Stalker, D. D. Despite a concerted effort to locate a copyright and a publisher for these works, none could be found. The Preface was written in September, 1909.

Chapter One

INTRODUCTION

Good morning. It's Monday! You have thirteen new messages. Please enter your password to retrieve your first message.

Nothing seems to change around here. More messages, more problems, more deadlines, and LESS time to reflect on God's perspective of my life as a Christian manager. If your situation is like mine, you'll spend more waking hours of your life in the workplace than anywhere else on this earth! Assuming that you relate to this, doesn't it make sense that the work force is where we should do the most to promote the Kingdom of God? I think the unequivocal answer is YES, but my behavior as a Christian manager sometimes demonstrates the opposite.

In recent years, it has become apparent to me that corporate America has become so "bottom-line" oriented that living a Christian life at work is often reduced to merely earning a living. The accelerating pace of change and the compelling desire to be productive have caused business managers to focus excessively on their products and services, while the effect of corporate life on their workers is scarcely considered.

While I don't believe God[1] would sidestep productivity, He would consider the life lived by His children (workers) to be a higher calling than business and its success. His passion would be found in promoting the Kingdom while laboring diligently in the vineyards (work force).

Jesus was the most productive person encountered by His disciples. He knew where all of the fish could be caught (on the other side of the boat) and how to erase all traces of disease from sick people left to their own demise. As a manager, He chose a work force of twelve men who lacked education; some were even tainted with backgrounds of ill repute. Even with these handicaps, historical reviews show that His workers turned the entire world upside down; norms were questioned and miracles emerged spontaneously.

Perhaps the success of Jesus and His company can be attributed to the fact that material gain was willingly exchanged for spiritual gain to the Kingdom of God. His business brought that Kingdom to earth. It remains today, ready for a harvest of new conversions like the one that occurred to Saul on the Damascus road. The question of how to be a Christian in business is especially pressing for those of us who are Christian managers. Where can we turn for management training that has the Christian perspective? Every year thousands of business leaders flock to seminars on work force management. Seldom is mention made in these seminars about the Christian perspective. Perhaps, this is because no one has adequately discovered that God has much to say about Christians at work.

This book is intended to provide Christian management principles for business men and women who will add the Christian perspective to their management roles. It is written primarily for Christian managers who have a heart for work force evangelism.

The management strategies presented in this book have been developed in secular business schools and tested in businesses across America. What has been missing far too long is the rekindling of these principles with the Christian perspective. This book accomplishes that task. In addition, this book provides a user-friendly study of the *activities* and the *role-playing* of work force management.

Many business textbooks state that managers perform four basic activities.[2] Generally, the meaning of management activities is similar among those texts. In this book, however, four managerial activities are identified as Planning, Encouraging,[3] Organizing, and Controlling.

When explaining the "role-playing" of these activities, the term "manager" is used often. Clearly, the position of a manager is not limited to a corporate business practitioner, and it equally includes men and women. The intent of this book is to include pastors and Christian workers, professional business men and women, and students of management in the references to a "manager."

In these first chapters, an introduction to work force management is provided. The principles of management are being rethought from the Christian perspective. Specifically, early biblical accounts of work force management are given as a lead to introducing four activities of managers. We are encouraged to always be mindful of an opportunity to promote the Kingdom of God in these early parts.

In subsequent chapters, we'll look at two contrasting roles that may be chosen by any manager to initiate the activities of management: *Peacemaker* roles and *Taskmaker* roles.

The process by which these roles are chosen, in varying amounts, is called managerial "role-playing." Therefore, this book is written like a drama about role-playing the activities of work force management.

It is of utmost importance for us to comprehend the Christian perspective. It emerges when a Christian manager chooses peacemaker or taskmaker roles; the amount of either one being dependent on each unique management situation. It also emerges by role-playing the four activities of management in a fashion that is symbolic of a modern-day disciple of God.

Clearly, the essence of the Christian perspective is much greater than "Christianizing" basic principles of management. Throughout this book, reference is made to "the Christian perspective." The explanation given above and the highlight shown in **Figure 1.1** should not be forgotten by any of us.

The latter parts of this book will build a graphic model to visualize the dynamic roles of a peacemaker and taskmaker. This is accomplished by placing the activities of work force

Figure 1.1
The Christian Perspective

Christianizing
Principles of
Management

**Christian
Perspective**

management into a four-by-four "map" that results in distinct "cells." Each cell is then able to be activated according to the degree of peacemaker or taskmaker roles that a manager chooses. Also, I'll give a prescription for shifting between the peacemaker and taskmaker roles.

The information I offer will make you more productive and, more importantly, encourage you to promote the Kingdom of God while role-playing the basic activities of work force management.

Endnotes

1. *God* is declared to be omnipotent by the name *Lord* (Gen. 17:1; Ex. 6:3). His only son is *Jesus* who is the *Savior* of the world (Mt. 1:21) and referred to as the man Christ Jesus and also *Lord* (Lk. 2:11). God is ever-present as a *Holy Spirit* (Jn. 4:24; 2 Cor. 3:17). Throughout this book the deity of God is acknowledged by any of these italicized terms.

2. Textbooks often refer to these activities as "functions," meaning the four *functions* of management. *Activities* is the term being substituted throughout this book for simplicity and ease of understanding.

3. Some textbooks use the function of "leading" or "directing" rather than "encouraging." The intended Christian perspective in this book is the reason why "encouraging" has been chosen.

Chapter Two

WHAT IS MANAGEMENT?

Management has been defined as a dynamic process of achieving an organization's goals and objectives through the assistance of workers and other resources.[1] Examples of other resources include money, materials and supplies, time, and energy. This definition covers the critical factors shown in **Figure 2.1**.

Three of these factors are self-evident and will not have further explanation. It is necessary for me to elaborate on the critical factor that management is dynamic. This will be accomplished with an explanation of static ver-

Figure 2.1
A Definition of Management
Four Critical Factors

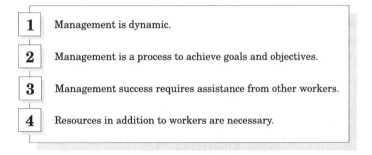

1	Management is dynamic.
2	Management is a process to achieve goals and objectives.
3	Management success requires assistance from other workers.
4	Resources in addition to workers are necessary.

sus dynamic processes in management.

Static Versus Dynamic Processes

An owner of a business records storage center once explained to me that a static process in his business is one that maintains an original space for a record (or box of records) that has been checked out. Nothing may fill the void space during the period of time a record is out because the storage process in this example is static. The space is kept empty, unused, because that space belongs solely to the record that has left the storage center.

This storage process would become *dynamic* if that space was not saved, but instead a returned record filled the void. In this dynamic storage process all records in the inventory would shift continuously.

Assuming an adequate tracking system, efficiency is greater in *any* dynamic process because all items are shifting in a crusade for improved efficiency. Even the rotation of our earth and the changing currents of its oceans are examples of dynamic processes.

The art of work force management is also a dynamic process because work force management involves people and other resources that are always in motion. This makes management a *dynamic process* of achieving an organization's goals and objectives through the assistance of workers and other resources, as I mentioned at the beginning of this chapter.

Management Input/Output Models

The dynamic management process is explained in some business schools through the use of a classical input/output model. **Figure 2.2** presents the model in its classical form.

Figure 2.2
Classical Management Input/Output Model

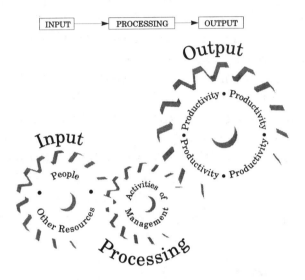

Three main components are evident in this classical model:

(1) *Input*—the employment of workers and other resources.

(2) *Processing*—the teamwork of those workers and other resources while engaging the activities of management.

(3) *Output/Productivity*—the end result.

An underlying notion of this model is that workers and other resources become companion ingredients which ignite a type of "processing" in order to produce the end result. To the typical manager, this result is usually some measurable amount of productivity.

For a Christian manager, however, this classical model is short-sighted. It suggests that management should result solely in productivity. It doesn't acknowledge that a business or work force may be favored by God to not only be productive but also to produce some beneficial gain to His Kingdom. Thus, the output of the classical model falls short for a person who desires to integrate the Christian perspective into the art of work force management.

An adaptation of the classical model, having components that result in Kingdom-Gain, is shown in **Figure 2.3**. Although I haven't found a mention of this adaptation in business textbooks, it is necessary for those of us who are willing to integrate the Christian perspective

Figure 2.3
Classical Management Input/Output
Model With Kingdom-Gain

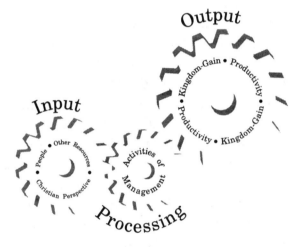

into our management activities.

One adaptive component in this second model is an inclusion of the Christian perspective as *input* to the management process. Another is the inclusion of Kingdom-Gain with organizational productivity as an output. We'll look at these in the following chapters. For now, the term "Kingdom-Gain" means to promote the Kingdom of God, especially at work. The effect of these ingredients is that output is measured in quantities of productivity and also in the amount of gain to God's Kingdom.

In further elaboration of **Figure 2.3**, it is essential to understand that components for Kingdom-Gain mean much more than just *what* the management process produces. The greater meaning includes *how* Christian managers use the dynamic process of management.

How a Christian manager finds organizational productivity *and* gain to the Kingdom is an animated portrait of his character. A Christian's character is the result of a lifestyle that is constantly transforming to the image of God. Transformation takes place by a renewing of the mind. Indicators of its presence will sometimes emerge through the voice and feelings of a Christian manager.

This character portrait is vividly displayed in the workplace during moments of adversity, because the way a Christian responds to adversity in a workplace (or anyplace) is a glimpse of his character. Hence, moments of adversity don't "build" character; they simply display the present form of character that, hopefully, is being transformed to the image of God (Rm. 12:2).

Congratulations! You've just completed Management 101. Remember, management is a dynamic process of achieving an organization's goals and objectives through the assistance of workers and other resources.[2] The transformation of your character is also a process that will be observed by your work force as you role-play the activities of management. The activities were defined in Chapter One. In the next chapter, I will provide an application for this discussion.

Endnotes

1. S. C. Certo, *Modern Management: Quality, Ethics, and the Global Environment*, 6th. ed. (Needham Heights, MA: Allyn and Bacon, 1994), p. 6. Used by permission.

2. *Ibid.*

Chapter Three

FOUR ACTIVITIES OF MANAGEMENT

As stated previously, our definition of management, including the Christian perspective, is "a process of achieving an organization's goals and providing gain to the Kingdom of God through the assistance of workers and other resources." In Chapter One we looked at planning, encouraging, organizing, and controlling. They are the four activities that ignite the process of work force management. Here is a definition of each one.

Planning	A process of developing performance objectives for each applicable worker according to his comparative strengths.
Encouraging	Offering motivation to each worker to conform to preestablished standards, while allowing the worker to work autonomously.
Organizing	Prioritizing objectives from management's perspective of relative importance.
Controlling	Measuring performance objectives against actual results and making corrective adjustments as necessary.

We will learn how to use these four activities to manage the work efforts (called "performances") of our employees. This involves six steps that are explained in this chapter.

Managing Worker Performances Using the Activities of Management[1]

The problems and drudgery of evaluating work force performances exist when managers and their workers do not initially agree on performance objectives and when performance criteria are not fully developed or disclosed prior to their evaluation. Therefore, the rationale for developing this six-step program is to equip us with a road map into "management by objectives" (MBO)[2] that can increase our productivity and profitability while remaining mindful of the need to promote the Kingdom. These six steps will enable us to conduct a symphonic choir with regard to work force management, rather than disjointed staff meetings with workers who, unfortunately, may be out of tune in their work efforts.

Workers need objectives to achieve peak performances and to curtail a possible alternative which is to wander aimlessly in search of appropriate guidelines for work. Infiltration of the Christian perspective can accomplish a meaningful gain to the Kingdom, as well as corporate productivity.

Here are the six steps to strategically develop performance objectives for workers. First, use the activity of *Planning* to develop performance objectives for each applicable worker according to his comparative strengths. Second, make certain each worker agrees that his objectives are meaningful and fair, while continuing use of the Planning activity. Third, use the activity of *Organizing* to prioritize objectives from management's perspective of importance. Fourth, use the activity of *Encouraging* to motivate each worker to conform to preestablished standards, allowing adequate time for autonomous work. Fifth, use the activity of *Controlling* to measure performance objectives against actual results. And finally, the sixth step is to implement rewards. Now let's look at the details of each step.

Step One: Develop Specific Objectives According to Comparative Strengths (Planning). The development of performance objectives that are tailored to each worker's strength is an essential first step. The nature of business often requires unique work and responsibilities among workers and, therefore, generic performance objectives may not be sufficiently productive.

Developing work objectives by concentrating on the individual value of workers is to maximize "comparative strengths." The principle of comparative strengths acknowledges that all workers are unique and, therefore, their degree of strengths and weaknesses will vary naturally among the work force. A concentration of comparative strengths means each worker has assignments and responsibilities that directly relate to his strengths. The desired strategy is to *maximize* each worker's strengths and to *minimize* his weaknesses.

Step Two: Agree on Objectives (Planning). Workers and their managers must agree on specific objectives, if critical success factors (CSFs)[3] are to be given adequate attention. In order to form an agreement, managers must first propose an initial set of tailored objectives to each worker. They should be convinced that the prescribed objectives are indeed fair. Negotiation and adjustments should occur until managers and their workers agree that, although the objectives are challenging, they are fair.

It is also necessary to answer in the affirmative this fundamental question: *"Can* and *Will* each worker, with some effort, fulfill his objectives?"*

Figure 3.1
The Fundamental Question

CAN and WILL ?

Further adjustments may be necessary until each worker agrees that his objectives can and will be achieved. When this occurs, there is no mysticism about desired performances.

Step Three: Prioritize Objectives (Organizing). It is not enough to simply agree on a menu of performance objectives. We must also explain the relative importance of one objective to the total (this, inherently, requires us to reward that what we say is important, discussed later). The best way to convey importance is to rank the objectives. Then, we should apply weights on a scale that equals 100 percent of management's expectations. Consider these hypothetical objectives for a typical worker:

(1) Create and maintain a data base of all customers who purchase brand X.

(2) Review order forms daily to assure they are properly completed.

(3) Determine other customers who could become additional users of brand X.

(4) Receive service calls from customers who have specific questions about brand X.

(5) Return all telephone calls by the close of the business day in which they were received.

These five objectives appear to be in rank order, yet they imply an equal (20%) worth of expectations. With the hypothetical weighted values shown in **Figure 3.2**, their relative importance is clearly illustrated.

Figure 3.2
Priority of Objectives

Objective Number	Relative Importance
1	35%
2	25%
3	20%
4	10%
5	10%

Step Four: Encourage Conformance (Encouraging). Now that performance objectives are clearly ranked and weighted according to relative importance, each worker should be allowed enough independent time to conform to standards while receiving encouragement from his Christian manager. If objectives are properly set up in Steps One, Two, and Three, a reverse appraisal is possible during Step Four. This means that workers would spontaneously approach their manager and ask, "So, how am I doing with maintaining the data base?" This proactive role of the worker is called "reverse appraisal."

Express a sigh of relief because the drudgery of evaluating performances has been removed. This is possible when workers and their managers have agreed to performance standards.

Other than casual conversation about performances and a lighted path toward the Kingdom from the Christian manager, a systematic review of objectives against actual results is necessary (Controlling—Step Five). The frequency of this review should be no less than standard employee evaluation periods: quarterly, semiannually, or, sometimes, as infrequently as annually. **Step Five: Measure Objectives Against Results (Controlling).** During a systematic review of performance objectives against actual results, a High/Low Achievement Scale could be used. **Figure 3.3** shows how to scale the achievement of the five hypothetical objectives previously mentioned.

Figure 3.3
A High/Low Achievement Scale

Objective Number	Relative Importance	Achievement
1	35%	High 100% — MH 80% — M 60% — ML 40% — Low 20%
2	25%	High 100% — MH 80% — M 60% — ML 40% — Low 20%
3	20%	High 100% — **MH 80%** — M 60% — ML 40% — Low 20%
4	10%	High 100% — **MH 80%** — M 60% — ML 40% — Low 20%
5	10%	High 100% — MH 80% — M 60% — ML 40% — **Low 20%**

Key: MH = Moderately High
M = Moderate
ML = Moderately Low

40

The highlighted areas on each scale show that this worker performed High on objectives one and two, Moderately High on three and four, and Low on objective five. **Figure 3.4** shows how performances would be scored using the sum of weighted averages.

Figure 3.4
Determining a Sum of Weighted Averages

Objective	Importance (A)	X	Achievement (B)	=	Score (C)
1	.35	X	1.0	=	.35
2	.25	X	1.0	=	.25
3	.20	X	.80	=	.16
4	.10	X	.80	=	.08
5	.10	X	.40	=	.04
	1.0				.88
	100%				**88%**

This worker received 88 points out of a possible 100 points, or 88 percent achievement.

Figure 3.5 is a sample, performance objectives form. The steps presented thus far are strategically placed on that form which synthesizes the entire performance-objectives model into a one-page report.

Particularly notice how the form requires two separate endorsements from the worker and the manager. The worker signs the *Agreement on Objectives* that is countersigned for acceptance by the manager. These agreements are made after Steps One through Three are fully implemented. The worker is then allowed adequate time and autonomy to conform to standards, receiving encouragement along the way (Step Four).

Figure 3.5
Sample Performance Objectives Form

Name: _____

WORK PERFORMANCE OBJECTIVES

TERMS, CONDITIONS, AND ASSUMPTIONS:

#	Objectives	A.) % Total Performance Priority	B.) Level of Achievement Results*	C.) A x B = C Weighted Value
1.			HIGH 1.0 MH .80 M .60 ML .40 LOW .20	
2.			HIGH 1.0 MH .80 M .60 ML .40 LOW .20	
3.			HIGH 1.0 MH .80 M .60 ML .40 LOW .20	
4.			HIGH 1.0 MH .80 M .60 ML .40 LOW .20	
5.			HIGH 1.0 MH .80 M .60 ML .40 LOW .20	
6.			HIGH 1.0 MH .80 M .60 ML .40 LOW .20	
7.			HIGH 1.0 MH .80 M .60 ML .40 LOW .20	
8.			HIGH 1.0 MH .80 M .60 ML .40 LOW .20	
9.			HIGH 1.0 MH .80 M .60 ML .40 LOW .20	
10.			HIGH 1.0 MH .80 M .60 ML .40 LOW .20	
11.			HIGH 1.0 MH .80 M .60 ML .40 LOW .20	
12.			HIGH 1.0 MH .80 M .60 ML .40 LOW .20	
13.			HIGH 1.0 MH .80 M .60 ML .40 LOW .20	
14.			HIGH 1.0 MH .80 M .60 ML .40 LOW .20	
			HIGH 1.0 MH .80 M .60 ML .40 LOW .20	

*MH = Moderately High,   Total = 100%   Sum = _____

M = Moderate,

ML = Moderately Low   Total Score = _____ %

Comments: _____

_____

_____

AGREEMENT ON OBJECTIVES   AGREEMENT ON RESULTS

Signature: _____   Signature: _____
        worker   manager

Accepted by: _____   Accepted by: _____
        manager   worker

Date: _____   Date: _____

After a systematic review (Step Five), endorsements are received for the *Agreement on Results*. This time the manager signs the agreement that is countersigned for acceptance by the worker, a reverse countersignature from the Agreement on Objectives.

Before the program is complete, however, we must implement Step Six—Rewards. This is not shown on the sample form.

Step Six: Rewards. If we fail to reward performances, we will fail to receive them again. Recognition and praise are examples of meaningful rewards. Our successful delivery of rewards will provide affirmative answers to these questions:[4]

(1) Were the rewards contingent on performances?
(2) Were the rewards worth the effort?
(3) Were the rewards equitably distributed?

The definition of "rewards" is seldom given by managers; often, it is assumed. Actually rewards are need-satisfiers, and they only motivate continued performances if they satisfy individual needs. Just as objectives should differ among workers, due to comparative strengths, so should individual needs differ among workers. One has to crawl into a worker's skin and walk around in it for a while in order to totally understand the worker's needs.

That, of course, is impossible, leaving the only permanent satisfaction to come from the Master of the Kingdom—God. Managing worker performance by objectives is complete when rewards are given that satisfy individual worker needs. Just like the results of the adapted input/output model explained in Chapter Two, business productivity and gain to the Kingdom can both result from this program. What better outcome could we expect? Tragically, some Christian managers will fail to offer the only true satisfier, the only true motivator for a work force, which is a touch from God, the Master of all and the vivid transformer of darkness into light.

This chapter developed further the four activities of management (planning, encouraging, organizing, and controlling). After giving a practical definition of each one, we saw how they could be adapted to a manager-worker relationship by using them to manage worker performances.

Following this six-step program does not guarantee that a business will always be on course for improved productivity and profitability, but according to an old adage, *if you don't know where you are going, any road will take you there.* For a manager with a Christian perspective that road could result in a gain to the Kingdom of God, only if the true solution to workers' needs is offered. That solution is salvation by God, forever and forever.

How to accomplish the delivery of Kingdom rewards is reserved for Chapter Six. First, it is necessary to provide an early account of management in the next chapter, followed by a discussion about the Kingdom of God.

Endnotes

1. Reprinted with permission from LAW OFFICE ECONOMICS AND MANAGEMENT, Volume 34, No. 1, published by Clark Boardman Callaghan, 155 Pfingsten Road, Deerfield, IL 60015. Toll free 1-800/221-9428.

2. MBO—a program of setting objectives, devised by management scholar Peter Drucker. At the root of MBO is the recognition that every person and every job in an organization exist for a reason.

3. CSFs are those activities most critical to achieving objectives.

4. James M. Higgins, *Human Relations Concepts and Skills* (New York: Random House, 1982), p. 71. Used by permission.

Chapter Four

AN EARLY ACCOUNT OF MANAGEMENT

Principles of management did not originate in modern business schools. An early account of an attempt to improve management is recorded in the Book of Exodus,[1] Chapter 18. We will review that passage of a management encounter between Jethro and Moses in storybook fashion.

The scene begins with Jethro, a priest of Midian who had seven daughters. After meeting and assisting Jethro's daughters by drawing water for a flock of sheep, Moses eventually became Jethro's shepherd and the husband of his daughter, Zipporah.

On one occasion Moses led Jethro's flock to the far side of a desert that ended at a place called Horeb, the Mountain of God. Here Moses experienced a call from God to deliver Moses' people, Israel, from slavery in Egypt. This call was so compelling that Moses went to Jethro and asked if he could return to his people (in Egypt) in order to see if any of them were still alive. Jethro was taken with compassion for God's call to his son-in-law and granted permission for Moses to return.

After time passed, Jethro heard that through Moses' leadership, God had brought Israel out of the spiteful hands of the Egyptians (Ex. 18:1). Having learned that Moses was camped in the wilderness at the Mountain of God, Jethro sent word to Moses that he, along with Zipporah and her two sons, was coming to visit and rejoice (Ex. 18:5).

As Moses and Jethro were reviewing God's deliverance of Israel, Jethro intuitively realized that Moses had become nearly all things to all of his people. Not only was Moses the supreme counsel in regard to managing interpersonal relationships among the Israelites, he was also making all of the general business decisions (Ex. 18:14).

Being a man of wisdom, Jethro told Moses in specific terms that it was not right for him to manage all of the affairs of his people single-handedly (Ex. 18:17). "Find some reputable and capable men," advised Jethro, "and make them judges." (20th century corporate America would call these judges "managers.")

An Organizational Chart. "Here is a better managerial structure," Jethro must have explained. "Have one judge *(director)* for one thousand people and then have ten judges *(managers)* under their span of control, each one in charge of 100 people. Each of these judges (managers) should have two judges *(supervisors)* who are responsible for the affairs of 50 people. Finally, Jethro prescribed five judges *(coordinators)* for each judge that has been described here as a supervisor, and each one should be responsible for the affairs of ten people."

Figure 4.1
Jethro/Moses – An Organizational Chart

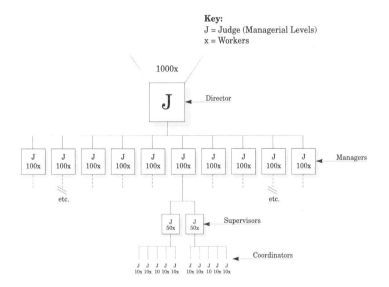

Only those matters that were extremely complex or of utmost importance were to be dealt with by Moses himself. The small matters were to be properly resolved by leaders under Moses.

Hierarchy of Authority. Although he would not have thought in these terms, Jethro was prescribing to Moses a contemporary hierarchy for a manager's span of control. That hierarchy is shown in **Figure 4.2** as a ladder to represent work force positions.

Figure 4.2
Ladder of Hierarchy

A definition of the positional rights of each step follows:

Director   A worker having the positional right to direct and assist leaders who possess managerial authority, supervisory authority, or coordinating authority, and the right to make decisions that affect the strategic affairs of the organization.

Manager   A worker having the positional right to direct and assist supervisors and coordinators regarding the work-related behavior of subordinate workers.

Supervisor   A worker having the positional right to direct the efforts of workers and coordinators to achieve the divisional goals and objectives of their organization.

Coordinator   A worker having the positional right to coordinate the affairs of certain task areas, including limited supervision of the workers performing those tasks. This right is generally valid only for a designated amount of time that coincides with specific projects.

Worker A person who generally lacks autonomous decision-making authority, works individually, or participates in a team of workers to achieve departmental goals and objectives.

Reflecting on this management lesson from the Book of Exodus, the four activities of management seem to parallel those found in the management encounter between Jethro and Moses. Our modern business colleges and universities teach the same type of activities.

This raises the larger question of how secular and sacred management principles relate to each other. Basically, sacred management principles contain the Christian perspective and they are applicable to secular organizations. On the other hand, secular management principles are often in conflict with the desired management roles that Christian managers choose.

The distinct difference between secular and sacred management principles originates with a practical adaptation of the classical input/output model, as explained in Chapter Two. The sacred adaptation adds a Christian's perspective to the input process of management. Once this added ingredient is processed, the output results in productivity *and* gain to the Kingdom.

Therefore, it can be said that the Christian perspective transforms secular management principles. This adds support to the notion that the component for Kingdom-Gain means much more than *what* the management process produces. The greater meaning includes *how* Christian managers use the dynamic process of management.

Endnotes

1. L. W. Rue and L. L. Byers, *Management Theory and Application*, 4th. ed. (Homewood, IL: Richard D. Irwin, 1986), p. 8. A refreshing but abbreviated account of this biblical passage is found in this textbook.

Chapter Five

MANAGEMENT AND THE KINGDOM

*The Kingdom on earth is the reign of God
in individual hearts.*
– James Stalker, 1909

Using the term "Kingdom-Gain" enables us to broaden our thoughts about God's Kingdom. It is more than a destiny for saints who have died. It is even more than an everlasting Kingdom of Heaven.

Equating the Kingdom of God with Heaven obscures the simple truth that God's Kingdom is spiritual in nature, "found wherever the will of God reigns in the individual hearts of Christians.[1]" While the Kingdom of God is evidenced in Heaven, we find it here on earth—even in our workplaces, role-played through the activities of managers who have the Christian perspective.

The purpose of His earthly Kingdom is to tell the redemptive story of salvation. When a guilty sinner receives salvation, a certain "gain" has been added to the Kingdom of God. It amounts to another person who previously wandered aimlessly in search of material satisfaction having found God, and through Him, received the gift of life everlasting.

Explanation of Kingdom-Gain

In our context, the term Kingdom-Gain means that a Christian manager can also achieve "gain" for the Kingdom of God in addition to organizational productivity. One of the ways this occurs is when workers see a glimpse of God through the role-playing of their Christian manager. Phantom faces of organizational success fall pale before the complexion of God that should be illuminated in a Christian's heart. To the extent this happens, God's Kingdom on earth finds immediate gain.

This discussion is clearly a portrait of Kingdom-Gain. It is the essence of God, the purpose of Christians' "call" to work force management, the ultimate measure of their success, and the highest dividend ever to be paid. Indeed, Kingdom-Gain is the spread of the gospel. The story below tells what happened when one manager carried the gospel to his work force, resulting in "gain" to the Kingdom. The story is followed by a further explanation of the Kingdom of God on earth.

A Manager with the Christian Perspective

This manager, fictitiously named Dale, worked at a mail order house loading and unloading mailbags from large postal trucks. The job wasn't exciting to Dale, but he worked hard and his bosses took notice. From outward appearances Dale was a model worker. On the inside, however, a spiritual struggle was building momentum. Dale wanted to share his secret faith in God with other workers but lacked courage.

Dale prayed relentlessly for a spiritual driving force that would cause him to share his Christian faith. Then, one day Dale's boss asked him to become the warehouse manager in charge of inventory control. He accepted, knowing clearly that God heard his prayer and was about to send him into that warehouse to share Jesus with every worker.

The first day as a manager was life-changing for Dale. Walking into the inventory warehouse, he was suddenly surrounded by total quietness—like the sound of a bird flying high across the sky. There was no trail of anyone having been there before.

"Hellooo," yelled Dale. "Anybody here?" he continued. No answer. "Where are the people who will love Jesus more?" Dale asked God under his breath. The answer wasn't audible but God's Spirit convinced Dale that his witness would not fall on deaf ears.

"Over here," someone said faintly. "Where?" asked Dale. "In the back," was the reply. "My name is Glenn, and I'm the warehouse director. There are no other workers but you and me," exclaimed the voice from a distance.

Suddenly, Dale's eyes focused on the director named Glenn who was smoking marijuana. Once Dale drew closer, Glenn proceeded to introduce himself as a former college professor. He recently suffered a nervous breakdown and believed in the Buddhist faith for answers about life.

Dale was speechless. Could it be possible that Dale's promotion was divine providence for the Christian perspective to be shown to Glenn? Indeed, it was. God had a plan, and Dale was to become the leading character to carry the gospel to a work force consisting solely of a director named Glenn.

Dale and Glenn spent countless hours together, counting mail and telling life stories. It was during that time together when Glenn asked Dale why he seemed to be at peace and why he was always happy. Dale knew this was

God's timing. Without hesitation, he explained that Jesus was his source of peace and happiness.

The days that followed included lunch hours spent talking about Jesus and the Bible. Dale couldn't answer all of Glenn's questions about God, but Dale's honesty caused Glenn to trust him completely.

After several months of conversation, friendship and sharing God's word, Glenn accepted Christ as his Savior. Now he is part of God's Kingdom on earth!

As for Dale, he entered full-time Christian ministry in youth evangelism. Today, he serves as Assistant Pastor for Youth at a large Christian and Missionary Alliance Church. Many teenagers are added to the Kingdom each year as a result of Dale's vibrant ministry. This story is evidence of what the Christian perspective can do in the lives of managers.

God used Dale to bring Glenn into His Kingdom, and Glenn was used to strengthen the courage and faith of Dale. This story has been told to encourage those of us who are Christian managers and who have a desire to carry the Christian perspective to our work force. God knew all along that you and I would be affected by Dale's evangelistic role. In order for all of us to have benefitted, it was necessary for Dale to have an evangelistic heart for Glenn. I'm so glad he did!

The Kingdom of God on Earth

God's Kingdom is not limited to life after death for those of us who are Christians. It is also present here on earth, and we can initiate further gain. This Kingdom started with almost 120 men and women in the early apostolic church who prayed diligently for the gospel to spread. Subsequently, the Early Church increased to approximately 3,000 members on the day of Pentecost. By the time Jesus ascended into Heaven, the Early Church had more than 5,000 in its fellowship.[2] In the days following that ascension, further scores joined the Kingdom (Ac. 5:14, 6:1,7).

Even though the term "Kingdom" was used throughout the teachings of Jesus, it didn't originate with Him. The term was used earlier by John the Baptist, whose message was, "The Kingdom of Heaven is at hand." (Mt. 3:2) However, John the Baptist was not the originator of this term. Instead, "Kingdom" seemed to be part of the religious language of the day in which Jesus lived. As a result, Jesus was probably introduced as a child to language that referred to the Kingdom of God.[3]

Moreover, the term "Kingdom of God" can be traced to Daniel 7:13-27.[4] In that book, visionary prophets saw a great world Kingdom being preceded by the Kingdom of Heaven. Specific reference is made about a Kingdom on earth that will be inherited by saints (Dan. 7:18).

Author James Stalker reports the entire history of the people of God was founded on a conception of the "Kingdom."[5]

If the Kingdom of God is not limited to life after death for Christians, then we might ask, "When does the Kingdom come to earth?" It comes to earth when it comes to an individual by making entry into a soul that longs for a spiritual revival, even if encountered for the first time.[6] The Kingdom on earth is the reign of God and His power in individual hearts. Accordingly, Jesus said to His followers, "The Kingdom of God is within you." (Lk. 17:21) This Kingdom is known only to those who would believe.

In another account, James Stalker explains the Kingdom of God personally:[7]

The Kingdom announced by Jesus to be discovered is a happy one; and what these (meaning Scriptures) specifically suggest,as they are read over one by one, is, that Jesus meant by the Kingdom a spiritual principle, secretly and firmly seizing the soul, and pervading it slowly but increasingly as a leaven, until it has leavened the whole lump; it is a spiritual discovery, which fills the soul with joy and causes every sacrifice to appear cheap, if only the matchless price can be secured. In short, it is the gospel.[8]

A Christian who practices work force management can promote the Kingdom simultaneously while having responsibility for other workers. It is possible for management roles to result in organizational productivity as well as the building of the Kingdom. As Christian managers who believe that God's grace is sufficient for achieving both productivity and for advancing His Kingdom, this dual outcome must be our goal.

The Kingdom of God within a Work Force

God's Kingdom is a source of power that can be used to touch needy souls in a work force. Mark 9:1 acknowledges that some Christians will not taste death until they have seen the Kingdom of God come with its power! That Kingdom and transforming power will be seen in a workplace by managers who display the Christian perspective when role-playing our established activities of management. But once again, it is available only to those who would believe.

Such belief is long overdue, and it must be accompanied by a passion to integrate the Christian perspective into work force management. Who will hear the call? The harvest is a work force that is ripe for the cultivating ways of a Christian manager having the Christian perspective. Will you be the one?

A pastor or other Christian worker, a business person, or a student of management can learn not only to achieve organizational productivity, but can also find Kingdom-Gain by realizing that the Kingdom of God lies within a Christian. The more conversions that occur in a work force, the more gain to the Kingdom.

Workers' Individual Needs. Business studies conclude that all workers have individual needs. **Figure 5.1** outlines three propositions about their needs.

There is a reason why all workers have

Figure 5.1
Three Propositions about Worker Needs

1. All workers have needs.

2. Managers don't have answers for their workers' deepest needs.

3. What workers believe they need today will change tomorrow.

needs, why managers don't have answers for their deepest needs, and why workers' needs change constantly. Nothing material can totally satisfy human needs. They can only be quenched by God, by His life-changing presence in the lives of His harvest workers and by His transforming power. Workers believe they need power; God offers peace through surrender. Workers believe they need money; God offers contentment. Workers believe they need affiliation; God offers unconditional and never ending love for all who would reach for His hand. Workers believe they need rights; God offers grace.

In further elaboration, there is a measurable difference between human rights and God's grace. First, human rights are finite, such that an all-inclusive Bill of Rights has been prepared by law makers for us to follow. God's grace, on the other hand, cannot be measured. We know that God's grace reaches further than man's greatest sin.

The object of grace is to restore and not to destroy, according to Dr. Bert Anderson, a Baptist General Conference preacher and administrator of many years. God's grace doesn't necessarily remove consequences of wrongful actions, but it does provide a means for restored fellowship with Him. While workers search continuously for need satisfiers, God waits for those who need restoration in their lives. His touch is a permanent solution, without any means for reimbursement.

An example of needs being truly satisfied is given by an account of apostles Peter and John who were going up to the Temple mid-afternoon one day to pray (Ac. 3:1-10). There were nine gates into the Temple, and a crippled beggar was usually situated at the gate called "Beautiful," believed by many authorities to be the "Eastern Gate.[9]" When Peter and John approached this Eastern Gate "Beautiful," Peter told the beggar that neither he nor John had any money. Although the beggar believed he had a need for money, Peter realized that a touch from Jesus was the real need. Therefore, in the name of Jesus, Peter commanded the beggar to get up and walk.

Upon being miraculously healed, the beggar began praising Jesus for this healing miracle. Although the beggar thought he needed money, he found complete satisfaction from the healing power of Jesus. The Kingdom must have realized tremendous gain from the healing of this beggar. All those who watched were speechless.

You see, only God can satisfy our needs. Short of His touch, workers, no matter how well off materially, will always search for "need" satisfaction. The search occurs at every workplace where collectively thousands of workers gather daily. Some of them are at the Gate "Beautiful," and they may not even know it.

The following illustration tells about a modern-day worker who was crying at the Gate Beautiful. He thought something material would quench a compelling need, but ultimately God became the only source of satisfaction.

A Modern-Day Worker Crying at the Gate

Just a few days before Christmas the manager's secretary picked up an incoming call. "It's the police department calling," she said to the manager. Continuing, she said . . .

You need to go to the county jail and sign some papers because they have appre hended a thief who illegally entered our computer room last night and stole two computers. He worked for the mainte nance company and had a master key. He was caught trying to pawn the com puters for Christmas money in order to purchase toys for his kids.

Fortunately for this sinner, the manager was a Christian with a burning passion for promoting God's Kingdom. "Before I sign anything," said the manager to the detective on the telephone, "I want to talk to this person." (Call him Randy.)

"Well, OK," said the detective, "but please don't dismiss the charges; he has confessed to the crime and belongs in jail."

Although Randy was indeed a thief, this manager saw a depressed sinner who was searching for ways to satisfy a deep need for his family to experience a joyful Christmas. *People without a relationship with Jesus would naturally desire material substitutions for the joy of Christmas,* thought the manager. *Randy doesn't need toys for his children. What he really needs is to receive Jesus as Lord of all! Amazingly, His presence is a gift that is totally free. Randy has broken the law while crying at the Gate Beautiful!*

The discussion with Randy was like viewing the cumulative effects of sin on the life of a destitute worker. This view caused the manager's eyes to squint, as if looking through a fogged window some distance away from where he stood. Inside the imaginary oblique glass was the shadow of evil, its tormenting lashes and the gestures of a fellow worker who had lost all purpose for life. Randy didn't resist any potential consequences for his crime. His depression would have welcomed the worst.

The detective pleaded with the manager to press charges. Another person said that jail would be the best help for Randy. The company president reprimanded the manager for his decision. Even Randy listened with a startled look of helplessness. "I want him to be released," said the manager to the detective.

"Randy, I want you to meet me in my office first thing tomorrow morning to make things right," continued the manager. The authorities shook their heads and claimed this to be Randy's lucky day. But it wasn't. Startled and humbled by this episode, Randy promised to meet the manager in the morning for restitution. He kept his promise. Randy brought his wife along for this awkward meeting with the manager who granted his freedom. The meeting began with piercing silence. Who would say the first word? The manager would, and he made the following statement:

The reason that I didn't press charges is I realize your family must have some great needs. I want to tell you something that you probably won't understand. Even if you hadn't been caught stealing, the money from a pawn shop would not have satisfied your needs.

I wish that you could know the Savior as I know Him. Then you would find sat isfaction. Yes, that means I'm talking religion. You see, I'm a Christian, and I believe this awkward situation can be used to introduce you to God's Kingdom.

What I ask in restitution for what you did, Randy, is for you and your wife to attend my small group meetings held each Sunday night at 6:00 p.m. They last for only one hour. Our facilitator's name is Mrs. Wilson, and she is leading us through a study in the Book of Mark— one of the books in the Bible.

This was Randy's lucky day. He was being directed to the only permanent satisfier of human needs. The Kingdom was being viewed by a thief!

Randy and his wife have a developing interest in church. I don't know if a conversion has taken place, but Randy's life (his wife's, too) is being changed week by week. This is another life illustration of Kingdom-Gain.

The term Kingdom-Gain is used extensively throughout this book to remind Christian managers of the ever-present opportunity to influence their work force so that, in addition to productivity, a measurable gain can result in God's Kingdom on earth. Only managers with the Christian perspective can effectuate such a gain because these managers are of "good seed" (Mt.13:38) and, in addition to productivity, have an evangelism role for initiating Kingdom-Gain.[10]

Endnotes

1. James Stalker, *The Ethic of Jesus* (New York: Eaton & Mains, 1909).

2. Warren W. Wiersbe, *Be Dynamic* (Wheaton, IL: Victor Books, 1987), p. 51. Used by permission.

3. Stalker, *op. cit.*, p. 42.

4. *Ibid.*

5. *Ibid.*

6. *Ibid.*, p. 26.

7. *Ibid.*, p. 30.

8. Dr. James Stalker was indeed a prolific writer during the turn of the century. His works are scarcely found today. The truth and practicality of his writings simply could not be passed from inclusion in this management book. Other books written by Stalker in the early 1900s include the following:
(1) *The Ethic of Jesus According to the Synoptic Gospels;*
(2) *Imago Christ: The Example of Jesus;*
(3) *The Preacher and his Models;*
(4) *The Trial and Death of Jesus Christ: A Devotional History of our Lord's Passion;*
(5) *The Christology of Jesus: Being His Teaching Concerning Himself According to the Synoptic Gospels;*
(6) *The Atonement.*

9. Wiersbe, *op. cit.*, p. 37.

10. For additional readings about God's Kingdom, see the
following texts:
    (1) Charles Colson with Ellen Santilli Vaughn,
        Kingdoms in Conflict (New York: Inspirational
        Press, 1987).
    (2) Tony Campolo, *The Kingdom of God is a Party*
        (Dallas, TX: Word Publishing, 1990).

Chapter Six

R$_X$: FOOTPRINTS TO FOLLOW

Up to this point four activities of management have been introduced, followed by applications. The need to promote the Kingdom when managing a work force has been established. It is not enough, however, to simply express the need for evangelism at work. This chapter goes a step beyond and provides two prescriptions that teach a Christian manager "how to do it."

These prescriptions were first developed by Kingdom "heroes" who are living testimonies of work force evangelism. They have hands-on business experience. I am calling these prescriptions, *"Footprints to Follow."* They have been written to encourage readers of this book. Each Rx is preceded by a biographical sketch and a business venture.

Footprints to Follow

Dr. R. Stanley Tam[1]

Biographical Sketch. I have been wonderfully blessed by God to have traveled around the world speaking in over twenty-five mission fields. Within the United States I have been equally privileged to teach God's message over seven thousand times at churches, conferences, retreats, mayors' prayer breakfasts, and civic clubs.

Additionally, I have served on the International Board of Managers of The Christian and Missionary Alliance, and the Youth for Christ International Board. I have also been elected by my own church as Elder for life.

Concerning my businesses, I serve as President of both the United States Plastic Corporation and the United States Smelting and Refining Corporation, which have some eighty-four thousand customers. Also, I serve as Board Chairman of Tamco Industries, Incorporated.

It is my delight to travel on weekends holding "God Owns My Business" seminars and general conferences that explain how a person can become a soul winner. The essence of these seminars and conferences is the following: (1) how to run a successful business, (2) how to put Christ in your business, and (3) how to eliminate problems in your business and Christian life.

A Memorable Business Venture. Several years ago I came into a milestone business encounter with God, which I shall never forget. I gave God's closing message at a series of revival meetings in Columbia, South America, one Saturday night to a sparse crowd in a half-filled sanctuary.

Some people were coming to the altar to meet God. I couldn't sit down because I felt the presence of the Holy Spirit so strongly right where I stood—behind the pulpit! For a few moments my every thought, gesture, and passion became focused on my Redeemer. The crowd probably thought I was praying for the people who were kneeling at the altar.

"Stanley," I heard God speak in my mind's ear. "I want you to go back to Ohio and turn your entire business over to Me so that others might know Me like you do."

Well, God, You already have 60 percent ownership, do You really need it all? I thought to myself, *Why would God be asking for all of my business when most Christians won't even give Him ten percent of their earnings?* My attention returned to that Church service, but my heart pumped feverishly. I never before had such an encounter with God, nor have I experienced it again.

A few days later on January 15, 1955, I made my decision. I promised God I would no longer be a stockholder in either United States

Smelting and Refining Corporation or the United States Plastic Corporation. All stock would belong to Him, and I would be a mere employee.

One attorney refused to handle the transfer of ownership. Another said it couldn't be done. Yet, today God truly owns my businesses. They have become large and profitable. Well over a million dollars is given away annually.

This story about a memorable business venture is not a secret, and I'm honored to have it published in this Christian management book. A parable found in Matthew (Mt. 13:45-46, NKJV) tells why:

> . . . the Kingdom of heaven is like a merchant seeking beautiful pearls, who, when he had found one pearl of great price, went and sold all that he had and bought it.

A person's soul is the greatest value in business. Investing time in someone's life will pay dividends throughout eternity. The Rx that follows contains six suggestions for Christian managers who desire to use the evangelism roles of a peacemaker and a taskmaker to promote God's Kingdom at work.

Rx #1—The Work Force Prescription. I have taught soul winning for more than forty years, and my goal is to lead three people each day to make a decision for Christ. I suggest this six-step approach to evangelism in your management activities.

Establish yourself at the beginning of your career with a strong, clear-cut testimony that you are a Christian; then live it! Avoid constantly preaching or coaxing workers to accept Christ. If you nag, the work force will gang up against you, and you will never make any progress.

Keep all channels of communication clear. If you have any trouble (and you will) such as misunderstandings, or arguments, then humble yourself. Do whatever you have to do to make things right. It usually requires nothing more than an apology. If you don't make restitution when necessary, you will lose your credibility and will no longer have a Christian influence. Remember, the work force has a higher standard for a manager than does the Church.

When you hear that a subordinate worker is having trouble such as sickness in his family or other such difficulties, show kindness by taking over a pie or cake and say, "My wife (husband) and I are praying for you." You will be rewarded when that person comes to you and says, "You were the only person who showed such a kindness. What makes you so different?"

Offer an invitation to fellow workers to come to your office for a casual Bible study at noon. This is always in order, but should not be done on company time. The lunch hour is an ideal time for a casual study. Playing golf or tennis, or going fishing, are profitable events to break down barriers for unsaved workers to receive spiritual guidance. These events provide a temporary shield from telephone and office pressures that usually reside in a normal business setting.

Finally, don't push. Slowly draw a person to Christ. Your mission is to create a desire in that individual, without brute force. Love is the most powerful force in winning a soul to Christ, with dependence upon the Holy Spirit to complete the work.

These six suggestions have certainly worked for me. It is my prayer that this prescription will benefit you in your evangelism role as a peacemaker and a taskmaker at work. An abbreviated summary of the six suggestions in this Rx are outlined in **Figure 6.1**. I have named these six suggestions "R. Stanley Tam's Work Force Rx!"

Figure 6.1
R. Stanley Tam's Work Force Rx

1	Establish yourself as a Christian at the beginning of your career.
2	Keep all channels of communication clear.
3	When you hear that a worker is having trouble, show kindness.
4	Offer an invitation to come to your office for a casual Bible study.
5	Use sporting events to break down barriers for workers to receive spiritual things.
6	Don't push; slowly draw a person to Christ.

Dr. Roy S. LeTourneau[2]

Biographical Sketch. When I was only ten years old, I worked in one of my father's factories. I learned to be an electric arc welder at that age. My father, R. G. LeTourneau, was the pioneer inventor, designer, and manufacturer of large earth-moving equipment. He was the first to put a large bulldozer on the front of a tractor and the first to put rubber tires on a tractor! Our family business was known as R. G. LeTourneau, Inc. We were the largest manufacturer of earth-moving equipment in the United States.

In 1970, the family business was sold. That same year my younger brother, Ben, and I acquired a John Deere industrial dealership with store locations in Orlando and Tampa,

Florida. Soon after this acquisition, we opened a third store on the farmlands of Ocala, Florida. Within three years, our dealership grew from the smallest to the largest John Deere dealership in the United States, possibly in the world! It was a business blessed by God, and His potter's hands were self-evident in that venture.

Then in early 1975, Ben and I sold our John Deere business. Ben moved to Texas, and I bought a Cessna dealership in Orlando, Florida. I personally managed that Cessna business for a couple of years.

The airplane business was as big a failure as the John Deere business was a success. Even though I lost money and at times was discouraged, I never doubted that God was in control.

For most of my life I have been involved with CBMC (Christian Business Men's Committee), which is a ministry of reaching business managers with the Gospel of Christ. I have served on the Local Committee, the Board of the National Organization, and the International Board. For eight years I served as Chairman of CBMCI, the international organization. Through these affiliations God has granted me the privilege of traveling to many countries of the world giving my testimony at business events and speaking at churches.

Money isn't a primary motivator for me. It never was, even though God blessed my overall business career with monetary profit. The life motto I subscribe to is one written by my father years ago:

> The question is not, "How much of my money am I going to give God"; the question is, "How much of God's money am I going to keep and spend on myself."

If indeed we are Christian managers, committed to Christ, then everything we have belongs to Him and we have to ask, "How much are we going to keep?"

A Memorable Business Venture. Building a section of road in the eastern jungle of Peru, South America, is a memorable business venture for me. That thirty-five mile road has become an avenue for many conversions, a tremendous gain to God's Kingdom.

It was spring of 1953 when I accompanied my father on a trip to Peru to look at a road project that the government requested. We agreed to build a 35 mile jungle road in an effort to open up a new area of the tropical rain forest. For payment, the government was to give us one million acres of jungle land that we intended to develop and sell off to settlers.

Our objective was to be Christian witnesses in the local area and to help evangelize that area of Peru. We called ourselves "Industrial Missionaries." Only committed Christian workers were invited to help us build the road and evangelize the local Peruvian workers. The task was most difficult since we had over 60 inches of rainfall a year and could only work half of the year.

On one occasion I made friends with a leading senator in Lima and had the privilege of leading him to the Lord in my office.

Another time, I was negotiating with Peruvian army generals to purchase some of their horses for our cattle ranch in the jungle. After finishing our business, they began to ask me about my father. Of course, you can't talk about R. G. LeTourneau without talking about the Lord. After telling them about my earthly father, I had the privilege of sharing the Gospel of Christ with them for nearly 45 minutes! I don't know if they entered God's Kingdom, but I do know that they heard the Gospel. All of this was possible because of a business deal to build a jungle road.

The Lord used my efforts as a work force manager to promote His Kingdom. I had never seen greater power of the Gospel before that business venture. I haven't seen it since.

Rx #2—LeTourneau Soul Movers. With a reflection on all of my past business encounters, three notions come to mind regarding the evangelism role of peacemaker and taskmaker managers. Each one is explained in the subsequent paragraphs.

As Christian managers, we need to be witnesses for Christ in *every* aspect of our lives. The way we live, the way we play, and the way we work are a witness one way or another for or against Christ. Your workers will not only notice your professional life, but they will glance at your broader life script. Just as a manager is sometimes a peacemaker and sometimes a taskmaker, a Christian is sometimes at work or at play. Curious workers are looking at the full script of a manager's life. Your total life actions will speak louder than your words.

Also, work force evangelism is not a stop-and-go event. This means that effective evangelism cannot be turned on and off with a toggle switch. Work force evangelism is a total way of life. It is living and working the way Christ wants us to and then taking the opportunities that present themselves to share Him with workers who are receptive. Actually, it is using the resources that God places at our disposal to further His work and His Kingdom.

The third "soul mover" says that a Christian manager *must* be fair and honest. How we choose to be a peacemaker and a taskmaker will be a reflection on Christianity. This doesn't mean that we shouldn't be efficient or that we should be a pushover. We should, however, treat workers with respect because it will open opportunities for us to evangelize the work force. How to be a fair and honest Christian manager becomes a natural process as surrender is given daily to the leading of Christ.

God has a will to be done here on earth (promoting His Kingdom), just like it is accomplished in Heaven. If Christian managers will not use the evangelism roles of a peacemaker and taskmaker, then who will make an eternal difference at work? No one—the mission field would be without a harvest.

We, of course, cannot force Christianity on our workers, but there are many ways that we *can* promote the Kingdom in a non-threatening way. This book is filled with illustrations and examples about how to promote God's Kingdom. To do so is to invest for the highest possible return—one that will last for eternity.

Figure 6.2 shows my Rx in a summary fashion, which I have named "LeTourneau Soul Movers"!

Figure 6.2
LeTourneau Soul Movers

1	A Christian manager must be a witness for Christ in *every* aspect of life.
2	Work force evangelism is a total way of life.
3	A Christian manager *must* be fair and honest.

Converging Footsteps

There is a common thread between the two prescriptions presented in this chapter. Work force evangelism is a spiritual process that takes initiative on the part of Christian managers. The Kingdom results are the responsibility of God. All that is required for Kingdom gain is a willing Christian manager. Promoting God's Kingdom is really nothing more than spreading the gospel of salvation, without force and without arrogance. It is not enough to simply express the need for evangelism at work. Taking action makes it a reality.

Endnotes

1. Although this information was tailored specifically for this book, it is partially replicated in the following text: Stanley Tam & Ken Anderson, *God Owns My Business* (Camp Hill, PA: Horizon House Publishers, 1969). See particularly chapter 13, pp. 95-99. Used by permission.

2. In addition to Christian work with emphasis on Missions, Dr. LeTourneau is an evangelist, conference speaker, consultant, song leader, and soloist.

Chapter Seven

MANAGERIAL ROLE-PLAYING

Not knowing his remarks would be written in a management book over 2,000 years later, the apostle Paul wrote letters to the Corinthians about choosing appropriate Christian roles. Prophetically, the apostle's letters illustrate a present-day need for Christian managers to fulfill the management role of a peacemaker *and* the role of a taskmaker with moderation in each one. His first passage is found in I Corinthians 15:58 (NKJV):

> Therefore, my beloved brethren, *be steadfast, immovable*, always abounding in the work of the Lord, knowing that your labor is not in vain in the Lord.

The second passage is found in I Corinthians 16:13,14 (NKJV):

Watch, stand fast in the *faith, be brave*, be *strong.* Let all that you do be done *with love.*

When combined, these two passages provide seven paradigms that are the successful qualities of a Christian manager who chooses a mixture of peacemaking and taskmaking roles. These paradigms or "high level directives" are summarized in **Figure 7.1**.

Figure 7.1
Seven Paradigms

1	Stand in faith
2	Do all with love
3	Be immovable
4	Be steadfast
5	Be strong
6	Be brave
7	Watch

The life of Jesus exemplified His ability to choose both the role of a peacemaker and taskmaker while breathing the virtuality of those seven superlatives. Hilarin Felder, in *Christ and the Critics*, stated the following passage regarding the qualities of His life:[1]

> We find in Him ardent zeal and inexhaustible patience, noble fervor and indulgent leniency, holy seriousness and sunny cheerfulness, an impulse to solitude and yet world publicity, majestic greatness and the deepest humility, inflexible determination and the sweetest gentleness, powerful energy and quiet self-possession, the warmest love for sinners and invincible hatred of sin, compassionate sympathy and strictest justice, irresistible attractiveness and fearless frankness, incorruptible truthfulness and extreme forbearance, mildness and force, resignation and resistance, adamantine strength and motherly tenderness, indefatigable outward activity and inward contemplation . . . and a ceaseless striving to promote the Kingdom of Heaven.

These qualities are a legendary account of harmonious taskmaker and peacemaker role-playing. Sometimes I wish we could have seen the actions of Jesus when He traveled through the marketplace. His were so very natural, flowing like an undisturbed stream of crystallized water, the type that is totally pure and refreshing for those of us who care to drink from His cup.

As managers with the Christian perspective, we will use the four activities of management by role-playing both a "peacemaker" and a "taskmaker" although in varying degrees. The emphasized role of a peacemaker is one of listening to the voice and feelings of workers, asking them questions, and making suggestions for improvement. The emphasized role of a taskmaker is to delegate, to direct, and to expect goal accomplishment (productivity) from

Figure 7.2
Peacemaker/Taskmaker Choices

Peacemaker
Listening
Asking
Suggesting

Taskmaker
Delegating
Directing
Expecting

workers. In isolation, they become the two extreme types of management roles.

The role-playing mixture that we choose is influenced greatly by the presence or *lack* of the presence of the Spirit of God in our lives. This presence is often referred to as the Holy Spirit. Where the Spirit reigns, there will be role choices that exemplify a burning passion for not only productivity but also for the progress of workers in their march toward the Kingdom.

If we would comprehend this notion about a Spirit-filled life, we would experience the sin in our lives being exchanged for the immeasurable grace of God. Where there is hate, God would sow love deep within our hearts. And where there is pride, He would exchange it for humility.

When every part of our hearts is cleansed by God, the best mixture of management roles (peacemaker/taskmaker) will be chosen. However, when our choices result in an inappropriate mix of the two management roles, a direct link might indicate a lack of the Spirit of God.

It is important to recognize that seldom will either role be an extreme behavioral choice of any Christian manager. It is natural for a manager to first assess each workplace situation and then choose to play varying degrees of the peacemaker and taskmaker roles appropriate for the intended results. Too much use of either role will make a work place disconcerting and cause role-playing to drift out of balance.

Role of a Peacemaker

Many Christians know biblical references to peacemaking. Romans 12 says, "If it is possible, and as much as depends on you, live peaceably with all men" (Rm. 12:18, NKJV). An implication of this passage is that whenever possible, peace should be made with all workers. Thus, an absence of peace among the work force should be an exception rather than a rule for managers having the Christian perspective.

The definition of "peace" differs between a Christian manager and a non-Christian manager. To a non-Christian, peace means the escape from immediate conflict and stress and the experience of an effervescent type of mental and emotional refreshment. To a Christian, peace is a non-escapest expectation, coupled with a reliance on God's sufficiency to provide our every need, while adverse circumstances sometimes remain unchanged.

To experience peace personally is to cuddle in the presence of God, like a child who finds the outstretched arms of a Christian parent during times of insecurity. It was *His* presence that Jesus was referring to when He said, "Come to Me, all you who labor and are heavy laden, and I will give you rest" (Mt. 11:28, NKJV). This is possible only with the presence of God, because an absence of conflict will be found only in Heaven.

Those managers who have peace are at rest

themselves and, therefore, can easily play the moderate role of a peacemaker when a situation requires emphasis of that role. Another biblical reference to peacemaking is found among the Beatitudes in the New Testament book of Matthew (Mt. 5:3-12). Specifically, verse nine says, "Blessed are the peacemakers, for they shall be called the sons of God" (Mt. 5:9, NKJV). To understand this passage, a manager must also understand the anatomy of a beatitude.

First of all, a "beatitude" is actually an equation. On one side is a certain condition, and on the other side is a blessing for those who are found in this condition.[2] Consider the verse that is quoted above as an example of a beatitude equation: "Blessed are the peacemakers,[3] for they shall be called the sons of God." The *condition* is to be a peacemaker; the *blessing* is to be called the sons of God.[4]

In a work force management context, the emphasized role of a "peacemaker" is to *listen* to the voice and feelings of workers, to *ask* questions of them and to make *suggestions* for improvements. Peace will be the wage paid to a manager who chooses a high dosage of this role, when it is indeed the appropriate choice. Thus, when a Christian manager chooses to emphasize a peacemaker role, he listens intently to the voice and feelings of workers, asks thought-provoking questions, and makes suggestions for improvements.

This discussion does not imply that a Spirit-filled manager will emphasize the peacemaker role above a taskmaker role. Only when a spontaneous workplace situation requires such emphasis should it be chosen. A Spirit-filled Christian should emphasize the role of a taskmaker when it is more advantageous to do so. Which role is chosen for emphasis should depend on the many one-time management situations that each business manager encounters.

Role of a Taskmaker

The epitome of an excessive taskmaker role is found in a drama about "bricks without straw," as recorded in Exodus Chapter Five. This drama intertwines with the previous management encounter that occurred between Moses and his father-in-law, Jethro. The main players in this scene are Moses, Pharaoh, and Aaron (the brother of Moses). While this story shows the ultimate destruction (of Pharaoh) that will result from too great an emphasis on the taskmaker role, we can also glean some positive insights.

Bricks without Straw

Moses and his brother, Aaron, went to Pharaoh saying, "The Lord God of Israel has said, 'Let my people go.' Therefore, Pharaoh, we request that you release Israel—our Hebrew people" (Ex. 5:1). Pharaoh, taken by surprise, claimed that he did not know the God of Israel and said that he *would not* release the Israelites (Ex. 5:2). "Pharaoh was unmoved either by God's authority or by human compassion."⁵

As a reply to the message given to him, Pharaoh concluded that since the number of Israelites had multiplied greatly they could produce even greater work (Ex. 5:5). Pharaoh, in his *excessive* taskmaker role, instructed his leaders to stop supplying the Israelites with straw for making bricks (Ex. 5:7). Straw was a major ingredient in the composition of adobe bricks.

The excessive dimension was that Pharaoh also mandated that their production quota be unchanged (Ex. 5:8). Any Israelite who could not meet his quota was to be beaten (Ex. 5:14). Pharaoh reasoned that by gathering their own straw, without declining quotas, the Israelites would not have slack time to worry about offering sacrifices to Jehovah God (Ex. 5:8).

Moses and Aaron delivered their God-inspired message to Pharaoh in anticipation that he would release the Israelites. Much to their dismay the bondage was intensified. In essence, Moses and Aaron were in pursuit of freedom but found only greater bondage for their people.⁶

Shortly thereafter, the Israelite leaders found God's messengers, Moses and Aaron, and asked them why they put a sword in the hand of

Pharaoh (figuratively speaking). Little did the Israelites know that Moses and Aaron actually pleaded for deliverance. The role emphasized by Moses and Aaron at this moment was of a peacemaker. However, the Israelite leaders, thinking Moses and Aaron had turned against them, confronted these two messengers with a heart-shattering rebuke. They essentially claimed life to have been easier before Moses and Aaron had come as messengers (Ex. 5:21).

It was at this point that Moses turned to God for reassurance of His calling (Ex. 5:22). Even Moses could not understand how his message to Pharaoh resulted in such a mess. However, God reassured Moses that although His message of deliverance had fallen on deaf ears and Pharaoh's reply crushed spirits, His deliverance would ultimately be experienced by the bitter and dismayed slaves.[7]

God's reassurance to Moses is the beginning of positive insights from this drama. This reassurance gave Moses the strength to continue to work for Israel. The story could not have ended any other way, for this was in conformance to the covenant made between Jehovah God and the Israelite forefathers.[8]

The drama of "bricks without straw" portrays the epitome of an excessive taskmaker. The excessive role of Pharaoh should never be envied by any person involved in work force management. There was nothing good about the role of Pharaoh in relation to the captive Israelites. Likewise, there was nothing good about the unfair treatment and bitter lifestyle that the Israelites experienced.

A positive insight from this drama is that a taskmaker's role has value to a work force, as long as that role is not abusive, vindictive, dictatorial, or otherwise excessive. The preferred role of a taskmaker is one of delegating responsibility, directing activities, and sometimes conveying an expectancy for goal accomplishment. When this occurs, the goals and objectives being pursued could also result in gain to the Kingdom. The appropriate degree of the taskmaker role for a Christian is to manage with Christian love and respect.

A benefit from emphasizing the taskmaker role is that certain workers would not find their true potential without that role influence. They would not find enrichment and fulfillment, and ultimately they would not be satisfied with their own productivity. Most workers need specific directives in order to focus their efforts toward goal accomplishment.

Moreover, the appropriate degree of Role-Playing a taskmaker is like the biblical account of leaven (Lk.13:21) where a metaphor is given about a small amount of leaven being able to expand a large mass of dough. The implication is that "a small influence will increase and spread rapidly."[9]

In closing, every manager has choices for the mixture of the peacemaker and taskmaker roles that are used in each workplace situation. A consistent Christian life will keep those choices in balance. For Christian managers whose choices are continuously out of balance, help is available if they are willing to change from the depths of the heart, through the infiltrating grace of God. This is explained further in Chapter Nine.

Endnotes

1. This passage was taken from a text written by Carl F. H. Henry in 1957, entitled *Christian Personal Ethics*. The original source has been traced to an early text entitled, *Christ and the Critics*, written by Hilarin Felder. The copyright © to this book is held by Burns & Oates, LTD in Tunbridge Wells, Kent, TN2 3DR, UK. Used by permission of Burns and Oates, LTD.

2. James Stalker, *The Ethic of Jesus* (New York: Eaton & Mains, 1909), p. 32.

3. Carl F. H. Henry, *Christian Personal Ethics* (Grand Rapids, Mich.: Wm. B. Eerdmans Publishing Co., 1957), p. 415.
   James Stalker believed that when depicting the blessed man, Jesus was describing His own character. The Beatitudes were wrapped with His own life.

4. James Stalker, *The Ethic of Jesus* (New York: Eaton & Mains, 1909), p. 31.
   According to James Stalker, the purpose of a beatitude is often misunderstood. The justification for "blessed" lies not in possession of a certain character but in the consequences of the blessing preceded by "for." If the term blessed is taken singularly then "Blessed are those who mourn" (Mt. 5:4) means "happy are the unhappy."

5. D. Guthrie, J. A. Motyer, A. M. Stubbs and D. J. Wiseman, *The New Bible Commentary, 3rd edition,* (Grand Rapids, MI: Wm. B. Eerdmans Publishing Co., 1971), p. 125. Used by permission of Inter-Varsity Press, Leicester, LEI 7GP, UK.

6. See *Guthrie, et al.*

7. See *Guthrie, et al.*

8. See *Guthrie, et al.*

9. *Guthrie*, p. 909-910.

Chapter Eight

A MANAGEMENT ROLE-PLAYING MAP

In the last chapter we concluded that with passing time, a skilled manager would choose both peacemaker and taskmaker roles. The degree chosen for either one is contingent on each unique workplace situation. Some situations require a greater concern for peacemaking than taskmaking in order to resolve conflict and accomplish production goals. In such situations, the manager would emphasize peacemaking roles. In other situations, a greater degree of the taskmaker role should be chosen. However, the extreme use of either role will be destructive to the work force and counterproductive to Kingdom-Gain. A "map" can be used to determine the appropriate mix of these two role types.

Basic Structure of a Map

Because a skilled manager will choose degrees of the peacemaker and taskmaker roles when using the activities of management (planning, encouraging, organizing, controlling), the two shifting roles can be envisioned in a bi-dimensional fashion. The interplay and contingencies of these two roles can be illustrated by means of a **Management Role-Playing Map**[1] (simply, "MAP"). For example, the shifting role of a peacemaker can be represented by a vertical axis, as shown in **Figure 8.1**.

Figure 8.1
Peacemaker—Vertical Axis

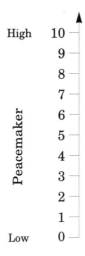

Similarly, the shifting role of a taskmaker can be shown by a horizontal axis, like the one below.

Figure 8.2
Taskmaker—Horizontal Axis

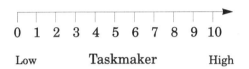

0 1 2 3 4 5 6 7 8 9 10

Low   Taskmaker   High

Since these two axes are scaled and since they have a common origin, as shown below, a converging scale "gauge" results.

Figure 8.3
Converging Scale

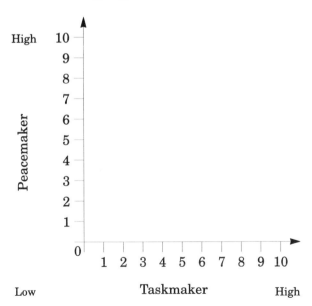

This gauge can be used for determining the degree of peacemaker or taskmaker behavior being chosen at any given time.

Referring to the figure above, a "9" on the vertical axis would represent a high degree of role-playing by the peacemaker. Conversely, a "9" on the horizontal axis would represent a high degree of the taskmaker role. This taskmaker "9+" role was wrongfully exhibited by the role of Pharaoh in the previous chapter. Would any one of us react like Pharaoh if put in a similar situation? Hopefully not.

Our management role-playing map can be more sophisticated when four distinct zones are created by joining the endpoints of a vertical and a horizontal axis so that a large box provides the framework of these distinct zones. Each area encompasses its own, complete square which is one-quarter of the space available in the overall map. The resulting enhanced management role-playing map is shown in **Figure 8.4.**

Figure 8.4
A Management Role-Playing Map

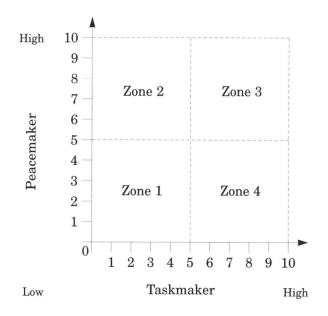

A Peacemaker and Taskmaker Role-Playing Map. Our map can be more enlightening by adding the four activities of management to the zones. The result is shown in **Figure 8.5**.

Figure 8.5
Peacemaker/Taskmaker Map

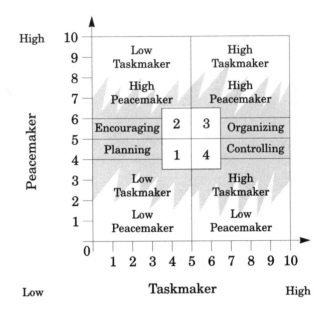

As you can see, Zone 1 represents the **planning** activity, having an equally low concern for making tasks as for making peace. This is because the activity of planning is generally outside of hands-on, work force and production management. Zone 2 represents **encouraging** which has a lower concern for making tasks than for making peace. Zone 3 represents **organizing** which has an equally high concern for making tasks as for making peace. Finally, Zone 4 represents **controlling,** having a higher concern for making tasks than for making peace (with adequate concern for both).

This map enables us to visualize a relative position found between the taskmaker and peacemaker roles as they relate to the four activities of management.

A zone in the map is activated when the quotients assigned to the role of a peacemaker and taskmaker converge and create a focal point. For example, in **Figure 8.6** the activity of organizing is activated when the quotient for a peacemaker (P) and a taskmaker (T) are both greater than five.

**Figure 8.6
Activating a Zone**

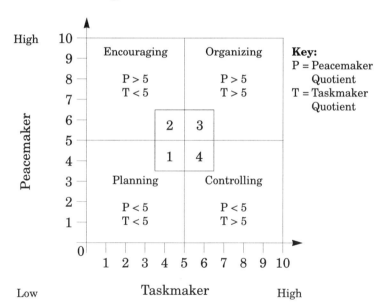

It is common for a manager to activate some or all of the four zones during a given workday while role-playing the activities of management. As a result, both taskmaker and peacemaker roles are necessary for skilled management. On the other hand, too much of either role can be destructive.

Shifting Management Roles
A further review of our map will show that Zones 1 and 3 are opposites as are 2 and 4. This contrast is shown in **Figure 8.7**.

Figure 8.7
Opposite Zones

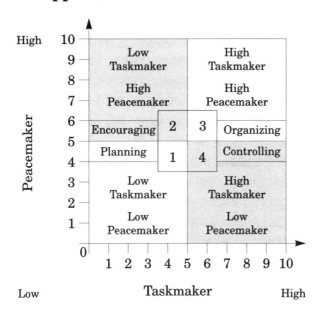

Zone 1 is planning, which represents equally low (but adequate) concern for taskmaking as for peacemaking. Zone 3 is organizing, which represents the opposite shift in behavior choice from planning. Notice that organizing represents as equally a high concern for taskmaking as for peacemaking.

Continuing, Zones 2 and 4 are likewise opposites in the figure above. Zone 2 represents encouraging, which has a lower concern for taskmaking than peacemaking. In contrast, Zone 4 (controlling) represents a higher concern for taskmaking than for peacemaking.

This role-playing map can be further expanded by means of a "stabilizing bar" that will enable us to study the way a manager can choose between the two role types. Shown below in **Figure 8.8** is the stabilizing bar, which resembles a bell-shaped curve that resides actively in the background of the four-zone map.

Figure 8.8
Stabilizing Bar

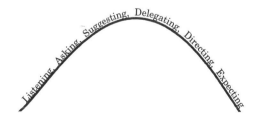

As we ascend the left side of the stabilizing bar, we notice the terms *listening, asking* and *suggesting.* These are the *actions* that define the role of a peacemaker, as explained in the previous chapter. Descending from the top of the bell to the right side of the stabilizing bar, we notice the terms that define a taskmaker— *delegating, directing* and *expecting.*

To shift from one zone to another on the map is actually a natural transition for a balanced Christian manager. He will shift from zone to zone throughout the workday in order to respond to many diverse and unexpected situations. The extent of the shift depends on the degree chosen for peacemaker and taskmaker roles.

A skilled manager will have a passion for role-playing a peacemaker and a taskmaker, although in varying degrees. A Spirit-filled life through God will enable this role-playing to balance, resulting in strategic maneuvers to benefit not only production but also the Kingdom of God.

Endnotes

1. Management researchers Robert Blake and Jane Mouton have used extensively a similar concept to this "MAP." Textbooks are replete with their account of "The Managerial Grid," which is to measure the feelings and values of a manager by expressing concerns for (1) production and (2) people.

Actually, the concept of a four-quadrant grid was initiated in 1945 by the Bureau of Business Research at Ohio State University in an attempt to identify the facets of leadership behavior.

The intended use and interpretation of the "MAP" presented here is quite different from these earlier accounts.

Chapter Nine

DRIFTING OUT OF BALANCE

Occasionally a manager drifts out of balance between the use of the peacemaker and the taskmaker roles. Drifting out of balance is a managerial ailment that can affect business managers, pastors, Christian workers, and students of management as well. When this happens the stabilizing bar, introduced in the previous chapter, can be used to help restore balance.

A Peacemaker Out of Balance. The following example of a well-seasoned headmaster, who accepted his new position at a Christian high school, will illustrate a peacemaker out of balance. There was a division between teachers who believed in total academic freedom and teachers who were advocates of censored curriculum. Academic freedom means the ability to teach without censorship of materials, content or applications. The new headmaster was fully aware of this division before accepting his position.

The first year of ministry at the high school was to be a period of peacemaking. With support from his directors, he was to promote peacemaking actions such as *listening to the words and feelings of the teaching staff, asking them questions* and *making suggestions for their improvement*. This approach seemed to work initially, and it gave him adequate time to investigate the essential nature of the division.

However, interpersonal problems between the headmaster and segments of the teaching staff became apparent after his first year of ministry. The headmaster became so accustomed to emphasizing the moderate role of a peacemaker that he drifted away from a balanced perspective into an *extreme* peacemaker role.

The faculty needed competent direction that would come from a balanced peacemaker and taskmaker. Instead, what they received continuously was emphatic listening, a few questions, and general suggestions from their headmaster. In order to resolve interpersonal conflict, the teaching staff needed responsible *delegation*, confident *directing* and some *accountability*. In short, the teachers needed someone to take control and organize the affairs of the school.

Unfortunately, their headmaster had drifted and was out of balance in his role-playing. Because he was out of balance, conflict among the teachers went unresolved. When teachers were divided over the issue of academic freedom, the headmaster would encourage them to set aside their differences and be happy. Often, however, the division intensified as individuals tried to resolve matters themselves without meaningful counsel from their headmaster.

Had this headmaster used the stabilizing bar to restore balance in his role-playing, rapport with the faculty might have improved. His remedy, under the leading of the Holy Spirit, would have been to choose actions that corresponded with delegating responsibility, precisely directing the activities of the school, and placing expectations and accountability on the teaching staff. These are the actions of a moderate taskmaker, found on the right descending side of the stabilizing bar. They are actions that could have restored balance in role-playing his four management activities.

Christian Workers Out of Balance. A second example will illustrate the reverse problem. In a large size church, there was a young couple, call them Wilma and Ted, who eagerly volunteered to start an innovative Vacation Bible School (VBS) program that would operate one night per week for the summer months.

Children through grade five were invited to attend. Wilma and Ted gave boundless energy to the new program, raised funds from outside sources to pay for art and craft materials, and worked harder than what most spectator saints thought was physically possible.

In little time, the results were astounding! The VBS program attracted scores of children, and many additional workers were needed quickly to manage the weekly program. It became the most populated curriculum in the church. Many children were introduced to The Kingdom as a result of this new format for Vacation Bible School.

The excitement and participation of VBS in this church grew immensely. Nearly every available worker in the church had some involvement. With regret, the pastor and the church board determined that many other areas of ministry were being neglected because too much of their volunteer-worker resource was allocated to this new VBS program. When Wilma and Ted were asked to share some of their worker resources with other ministries of the church, an episode of imbalanced role-playing began. Wilma and Ted assumed ownership of the workers and built a protective barricade and an emotional wall around their self-claimed program and workers.

Wilma and Ted quickly drifted out of balance. To make matters worse, they did not have a departmental leader who suspected this subtle but swiftly flowing drift. Protectionism caused their choice of behavior to become that of *extreme* taskmakers. They demanded respect and total commitment from volunteer workers; they chastised anyone who showed any resistance and verbally attacked the pastor for intruding on a successful operation of their VBS program.

Many workers became distressed. Some resigned from their responsibilities, while others became spiritually and emotionally hurt from the sudden and extreme taskmaker roles that surfaced from Wilma and Ted. This VBS program, which began as a wonderful addition to the church, became its most troubled activity. Wilma and Ted were not going to let go of the power that seemingly belonged to them from the success of their program.

Finally, Wilma and Ted were asked to relinquish their VBS responsibilities because no one could tolerate their extreme role-playing. Needless to say, Wilma and Ted left the church and caused other members to unnecessarily waver in their commitment to the church as well. The VBS program survived, but it required complete reorganization from new volunteer workers.

This episode could have been prevented if Wilma and Ted had only realized they were drifting out of balance in their roles. The stabilizing bar could have been a tool for restoring their balance. Unfortunately, Wilma and Ted never recovered. Scars of resentment, including shattered emotional feelings, lingered for years. Likewise, scars probably remained with the innocent pastor and other VBS workers. As this example shows, Christian workers *can* drift out of balance while role-playing the four management activities.

Restoring Balance. Balance may be restored by using the stabilizing bar to determine necessary corrective actions. For example, an out-of-balance taskmaker who desires to change deeply through the prompting of the Holy Spirit would emphasize the appropriate actions listed on the stabilizing bar to willfully move to another zone in the role-playing map. If balance was restored, they would have moved to the left side of the bar and would have subsequently corresponded to Zones 1 and 2 (Planning and Encouraging). The resulting emphasis is now on a peacemaker. This position can be located on the role-playing map displayed in **Figure 9.1**.

Figure 9.1
Moving Among the Zones

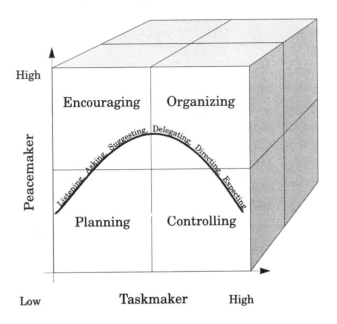

Using the stabilizing bar to move among the four zones will display the management activities that must be utilized in order to regain a balanced perspective.

During these days of corporate mistrust, the Christian perspective on work force management is deeply needed. There is also a need for Christian managers to be balanced in their peacemaker and taskmaker roles. Achieving this balance requires an act of the will, enabled by the grace of God. The stabilizing bar is a tool to make us aware of the occasional need to change actions from an emphasis on one role (peacemaker or taskmaker) to the other.

Endnotes

The two illustrations in this chapter, *A Peacemaker Out of Balance* and *Christian Workers Out of Balance*, do not represent any real situation known by or told to the author.

Chapter Ten

A CLOSING SCRIPT

Work force management has been redefined in this book with the Christian perspective. The previous chapters have challenged classical management thought. Writing especially for Christian managers, I hope that anyone can find road markers to personal salvation from reading this book. Before closing with an abbreviated summary and conclusion, just a few prevailing questions remain.

In posing these thought-provoking questions, I paint a visionary portrait of Jesus, showing up for work to say a few words to managers and workers. I will attempt to envision the peacemaker and taskmaker role of Jesus in this imagery.

What Would Jesus Do?

There's a contemporary phrase that asks, "What would Jesus do?" It's a relevant question for this closing script because if Jesus were present in the flesh today, He undoubtedly would visit a few businesses. What would He say about the effect of corporate life on His children? How would He react to corruption, immorality, inefficiency, game-playing, and the lack of contentment that prevails within many work forces today? How would He divide corporate profits? If He were in management, would monetary profits exist? These questions are answered as the probable peacemaker and taskmaker roles of Jesus are envisioned.

Upon entry to a modern-day business, I believe Jesus would oblige His Christian managers. Yet when He called them to righteousness, He would simultaneously glance at others who were living unrighteous lives. The beam of His clear, piercing eyes would focus on those who were loitering outside of the Kingdom. Just like He said so many years ago to the woman at the well, so would He say again to the ones who caught His eye, "Come and follow me, drink from my well, and you shall never be thirsty again." (Jn. 4:13) Talk about motivation! Life enrichment! What a promotion! Yes, His opening remarks would offer a fulfilling transformation to thirsty workers.

Just like a peacemaker, Jesus would walk quietly throughout the shop floors and gently touch the slumping shoulders of weary workers with the assurance that His Kingdom had waited for them. Only a few words would be exchanged, before the weary ones and the wayward sinners would understand the power of His divine touch. They would know that, although they had lost a foothold in their search for significance, happiness or prosperity, He was ready to lift them into the Kingdom of an abundant life that would last forever. Some workers would repent from only His touch. Others would find healing of lifelong scars of resentment, jealousy and corporate mistrust. The work force would know that Jesus had come; no particular introduction or explanation would be necessary.

"I am here," He would say softly to those who thought they had lost it all and didn't have a prayer. He would assure them that His love hasn't changed and He will always be with them, if they would only follow Him with their hearts. He would offer them love on a grander scale than they thought imaginable. He would promise that this love would never change, even if it seemingly came like a steady drizzling rain.

Indeed the squeak of His sandals would signify a tapping of workers to repent and to enter the Kingdom. Scores of workers and managers would respond, just as people did in the Bible stories. He would come as the Savior who walked the aisles of the Early Church. His compelling interest would be directed to those who had been passed for corporate glory and recognition, much like His interest was for the twelve disciples who formed His early company, referenced in previous chapters.

And just like a taskmaker, He would overturn the desks of those workers who were involved in corporate immorality. They are the ones who have defiled Him, using His name as a description of vanity. Frightened, humbled, and speechless would be those whose desks lay unsettled against the walls of the workshop. This is because the Savior, the Master of the Kingdom, had come to deliver His workers from mediocrity, unhappiness and from the sin that barricades their salvation. This impact would be so significant that it would become a precious moment in history.

If invited to a staff meeting, Jesus would talk about the need to work relentlessly for a fair wage and to take less than what had been given them. He would make it clear that the very purpose of life is to discover the Kingdom of God. Relentless work effort is an avenue for that discovery, especially enhanced, if the work force is garnished with the Christian perspective.

Furthermore, if Jesus were invited to a board meeting, He would address the officers about His definitive meaning of leadership. It would be understood that leadership is the consequence of servanthood. To be a great leader is to be a humble servant. This requires portraying the role of a peacemaker and the role of a taskmaker in varying degrees as the servant strives to touch the unmet needs of the worker by using the four activities of management. Sometimes this means emphasizing peacemaker roles. Sometimes this means emphasizing taskmaker roles, but all with the meekness of a servant.[1]

Before leaving the workshop floors, I imagine Jesus would remind all who experienced His visit to approach Him in the future like children. Children haven't wandered aimlessly in pursuit of a mirage of self-sufficiency. They are tender, needing the assurance and comfort from someone who has traveled before them. He would offer His continuing guidance for Christian managers who would become servants to the needs of a work force and who would call for Him to cross tomorrow's agenda with them, hand in hand.

His departure would leave a measurable gain to His Kingdom that exists in the hearts of believers. This Kingdom would be found wherever the perfect will of God was allowed to manifest.

Is it possible that Jesus has already come to a work force? He has come indeed if Christian managers have been in tune with the previous chapters and have committed to making a difference everyday at work! "Your Kingdom come, Your will be done on earth as it is in Heaven" (Mt. 6:10, NKJV), would be His prayer to God for each privileged Christian and wayward sinner who had experienced this very personal visit.

What About Profitability? I further believe that Jesus would be deeply concerned about profitability in any business that He may visit. The critical issue is understanding His meaning of profit! That meaning was articulated many years ago when He asked, "For what will it profit a man (worker) if he gains the whole world, and loses his own soul?" (Mk. 8:36, NKJV)

Jesus would review a balance sheet and an income statement only to determine how financial resources could be distributed in proportion to the needs of His children. Every manager or worker would have been paid enough if basic needs were satisfied. Any excess profits would be retained for the special needs of widows and orphan children.

As a living example of meekness and servanthood, Jesus would take far less for himself than any of us would deem appropriate. Nourishment and safeguard against terrain and other climatic elements would be the only exchange for which Jesus would accept wages. His basic needs would exist, but He showed no human desires for comfort and luxury. His head would bow in shame at those of us who sneak previews of material satisfaction.

Like the beggar resting outside the Temple, as told in Chapter Five, the Kingdom children need only the Master's touch, not paychecks that provide material indulgence. A little surplus may be appropriate for those workers having special needs, such as the crippled and those with other physical ailments. Outside of these examples, Jesus would have little passion for the value of wages.

Profitability—Yes! Profitable to the extent that each worker takes less compensation than work effort extended. It would be a higher value to be a worker, worthy of his labor, than to profit from manmade circumstances. Jesus promised that basic needs would be fulfilled for his devoted children, profit for more was never part of His inheritance. In our modern day, the sequel is to accept an employer's pay but keep only enough for necessities. The residual could go for Kingdom-Gain.

If Jesus built His first company with twelve unlikely disciples (managers) and literally unraveled the pillars of the whole world with a product of deliverance and salvation, would He be any less productive and profitable in a modern business situation? I think not! When He said that He would build His Temple, and the throbbing gates of hell would not be a doorstop

(Mt.16:18), he defined profitability. The measure is found in gain to the Kingdom. The commission for Kingdom-Gain has been repeated again and again throughout this book. The setting is a work force of people who are thirsty and ready for the harvest of redemptive salvation. Don't let the urge pass, YOU must have the Christian perspective on work force management! The Kingdom waits for you. How can you say NO?

Summary

Christian managers are the primary audience for this book, although we hope others will follow our journey. The flow of information has given a progressive development of the Christian perspective in work force management. The five critical steps that are summarized in **Figure 10.1** comprise this development. Each one of them has been discussed in previous chapters and is summarized in these closing paragraphs.

Figure 10.1
Progressive Development of
the Christian Perspective

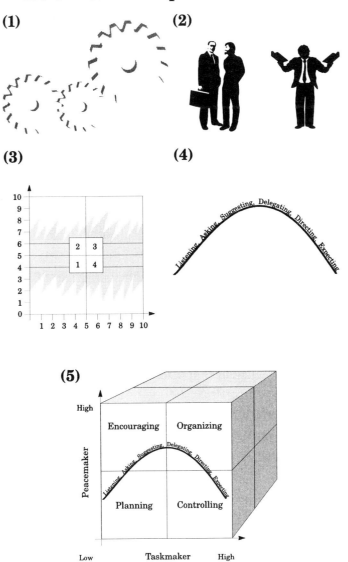

First, there were adaptive components to the classical management input/output model. One was the inclusion of the Christian perspective as an input to the management process. The other was the inclusion of Kingdom-Gain with organizational productivity as an output. The effect of these ingredients is that output is measured in quantities of productivity and also in the amount of gain to God's Kingdom.

The second step is to realize that all workers have individual needs. We as managers really don't have answers to their needs. In fact, what workers believe they need today will change tomorrow. Their needs can only be quenched by God, by His internal presence and transforming power.

Thirdly, the four activities of management (planning, encouraging, organizing, and controlling) were envisioned with a role-playing map that has four individual zones. Choosing degrees of role-playing, a peacemaker and a taskmaker will correspond to one of these zones. The management activity being emphasized will be identified by a corresponding zone.

This role-playing map was further expanded by means of a stabilizing bar which was the fourth step in the progressive development of the Christian perspective. It resembles a bell-shaped curve that resides actively in the background of the four-zone map. Ascending the left side of this stabilizing bar will reveal the actions of a peacemaker. Likewise, descending from the top of the bell to the right side of the stabilizing bar will reveal the actions of a taskmaker. If we are balanced managers, we will choose the roles of a peacemaker and a taskmaker, although in varying degrees. The stabilizing bar can help change the emphasis of those roles when necessary.

Finally, the Christian perspective can be balanced by moving among the four zones of the map in response to ever-changing needs of workers. This requires that the four-zone map and the stabilizing bar be used in conjunction with one another.

Conclusion

This book was introduced with the statement that workers will spend more hours of their life in the work force than anywhere else on earth. Therefore, the workplace is where Christian managers should do the most to promote God's Kingdom. All too often, the work force is void of having the Christian perspective included in the roles being played by its managers.

The essence of the Christian perspective is much greater than "Christianizing" principles of management. The Christian perspective can actually transform secular management principles. This transformation begins with an adaptation of the classical input/output model, as explained earlier and summarized below. When the Christian perspective is added to the *input* process of management, the *output* results in goal accomplishment *and* meaningful gain to the Kingdom.

Moreover, it is essential to understand that Kingdom-Gain means more than *what* the process of management produces. The greater meaning includes *how* Christian managers use the dynamic process of management. How a Christian manager uses the process is visible in words, expressions and mannerisms that are transforming the manager into the image of God.

The Evangelism role of Peacemakers and Taskmakers in work force management should be discovered and practiced by all of us. Among the questions that God will ask us, when our final day of judgement comes, may include, "What have you done to evangelize my Kingdom to workers on earth?" (Rev. 3:15,16) I hope your response is red hot. The best imaginable answer is to report that someone loves Jesus "more" because of your peacemaker and taskmaker evangelistic role.

Endnotes

1. Mr. John Smith, President of Trinity Leadership Foundation, teaches a transforming lifestyle through Spiritual Leadership. He has identified the following biblical passages regarding servant-leaders: Mt. 5,6,7; 20:25-28; 23:10-12; Mk. 9:33-35; Rom. 12; 2 Cor. 3:2-6; Eph. 4:11-32; Phil. 2:1-11; 2 Pet. 1:2-11. Used by permission.

About the Author

Dr. Bill McCallister is an adjunct professor of management and has a professional career in administration. He holds a BS, MBA, and an earned Doctorate in Business Administration. Through Nova Southeastern University, he teaches management principles on-site at Walt Disney World, Orlando, Florida, and at AT&T's corporate training facilities. Additionally, he has taught management courses at Harcourt Brace & Company, Warner Southern College, and Nyack College.

Dr. McCallister has a passion for integrating a Christian perspective into the study of corporate management. Thus, his purpose for writing this book.